D1141908

South Sefton
6th Form College

© 1983 by Ann Hutchinson Guest.
Published under license by Gordon and Breach Science Publishers SA.

All rights reserved.

First published 1983
Third printing with corrections 1995
Reprinted 2004
by Taylor & Francis,
2 Park Square, Milton Park, Abingdon, Oxon OX14 4RN

Transferred to digital Printing 2004

No part of this book may be reproduced or utilized in any form or by any means, electronic or mechanical, including photocopying and recording, or by any information storage or retrieval system, without permission in writing from the publisher.

---

ISBN 0-677-22310-2

YOUR MOVE - Chapter 1 Name:

Exercise Sheet - 1

## DURATION OF MOVEMENTS

List five everyday examples of movement which:

A. Use extended time; an uninterrupted, continuous movement of some kind.

B. Use short, quick spans of time; that is, separated actions in which use of time is interrupted. These may be single actions or in a series.

 Name:

Exercise Sheet - 2

## DURATION OF ACTION, STILLNESS

Notate actions and stillnesses of different durations:

A: In free timing for which no meter (time signature) is indicated.

B: In measured time spans. Indicate a specific meter.
(Draw in starting and finishing lines and bar lines.)

A

B

Exercise Sheet - 3

## TIME DIVISION OF A SPACE DESIGN

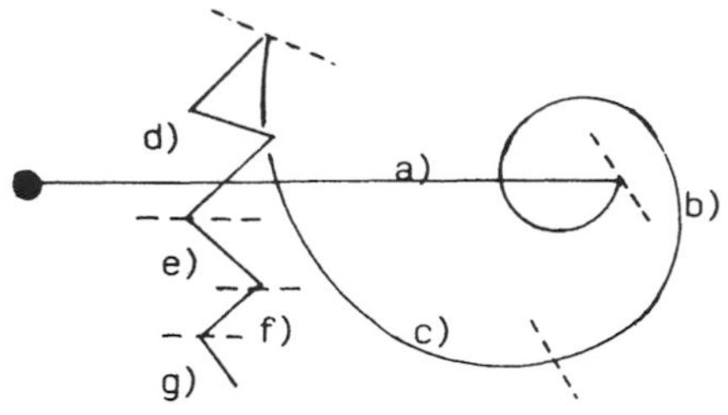


The spatial pattern here is from a Paul Klee picture. Draw it in the air with your right or left arm, starting at ● . You may add pauses where you like. Note that the design is marked off into segments, a, b, c, etc. as in the design in Ex. 8b. In the spaces below you have eight measures of 4/4. Decide how much time you will allow for each segment and for pauses between (if any).

Notate below the time you are using for each segment by use of an action stroke next to which is placed the identification of a, b, etc.

2 ______ 4 ______ 6 ______ 8 ______

4
4 1 ______ 3 ______ 5 ______ 7 ______

 Name:

Exercise Sheet - 4

## SEQUENCE OF ACTIONS - EFFECT OF DIFFERENT TIMING

The following simple three-part sequence is intended to represent greeting someone. This familiar sequence is performed in four ways, the difference lying in the timing. Match each version with the interpretation which you feel it best expresses.

A. Your greeting begins eagerly but it is not the person you expected. You then quickly turn your head in embarrassment.

B. A gracious greeting to a person you respect.

C. You hesitate before making a friendly approach to a person new to you.

D. A reluctant greeting to someone you would prefer not to acknowledge.

KEY

S = step forward

A = arm gesture foward

H = inclining the head

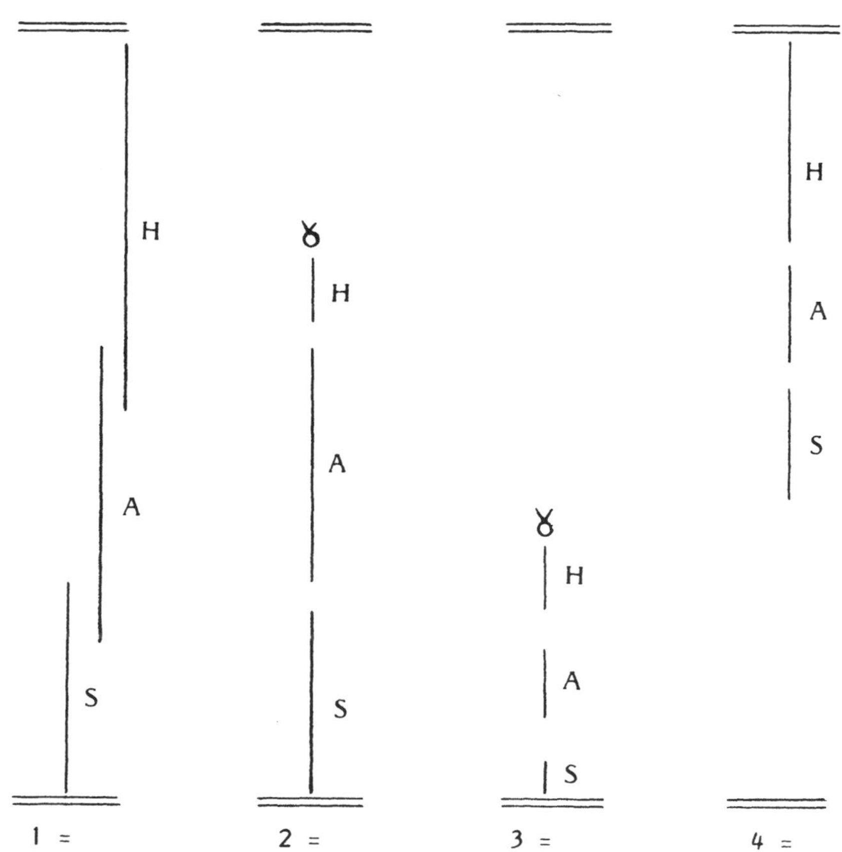


1 =  2 =  3 =  4 =

 Name:

Exercise Sheet - 5

## TRAVELLING

A - This section for those with ballet training:

Name six steps in the Classical Ballet vocabulary which must travel since they are never done on the spot. These can include steps which are usually repeated to produce extended travelling. Also list two examples for each section of B.

B - For movement study and contemporary dance students:

List four everyday activities in which travelling is usually:

1. Fast

2. At a medium pace

3. Slow

4. Passive a) i.e. you do not initiate the travelling. Also b) give two examples in which you travel without moving.

 Name:

Exercise Sheet - 6

## FORMS OF LOCOMOTION

Below is a list of words for different forms of locomotion. Describe what particular movement aspects (timing, energy, part of the body) each embodies. A few are answered for you as examples.

1. Cartwheel. Revolving laterally, supporting on foot, hand, hand, foot, body extended.
2. Careen (lurch). Unstable balance, irregular steps in size and timing.
3. Crawl.
4. Climb.
5. Dash.
6. Goose Step.
7. Jog.
8. March.
9. Promenade.
10. Rolling.
11. Saunter.
12. Shuffle.
13. Slither.
14. Sneak.
15. Sprint.
16. Stroll.
17. Strut.
18. Swim.
19. Swing (tree to tree).
20. Tiptoe.
21. Toddle.

Name:

Exercise Sheet - 7

## FORM OF PATHS

A. Notate the kind of paths used to produce this floor plan, i.e. circling, straight, meandering. Timing, step direction and distance are not important.

B. Notate the paths described in the wording alongside the staff.

Circle counterclockwise . . . . . . . Short straight path Stillness . . . . . . . . .

Meander . . . . . . . . . . . . . . . . . Straight path Stillness Straight path

A

B

Name:

Exercise Sheet - 8

## DIRECTION OF CIRCULAR PATH

Write the paths required and dance the sequence with the steps suggested to get the feel for the study, simple as it is.

| Steps | Counts | Steps | Counts | Steps | Counts | Steps | Counts |
|---|---|---|---|---|---|---|---|
| Run straight forward. | 1 | Galop left circling clockwise.......... | 5 | Walk forward circling CCW.......... | 1 | Galop right circling CW.......... | 5 |
| Run straight back. | 2 | | 6 | Turn left | 2 | Be still | 6 |
| Galop right circling counterclockwise.......... | 3 | Clockwise circle with forward steps | 7 | Walk forward circling CW.......... | 3 | Galop left circling CCW.......... | 7 |
| | 4 | Turn right | 8 | Turn right | 4 | Be still | 8 |
| | | Stillness | | | | | |
| | A | | A cont. | | B | | B cont. |

 Name:

Exercise Sheet - 9

## DEGREE OF TURNING, CIRCLING

Notate the appropriate instructions to achieve the given floor plans. Note the stated step direction and add turning as needed to face the required direction. Observe how each plan picks up where the previous one left off.

1 Forward steps travelling
2 1/4 turn right
Sideward left steps . . . . 1/4 turn left

3 Sideward steps to right
4 Stillness
Sideward steps to right 1/2 turn right

5 Forward steps . . . . . . . . 1/8 turn right
6 Backward steps . . . . . . Stillness

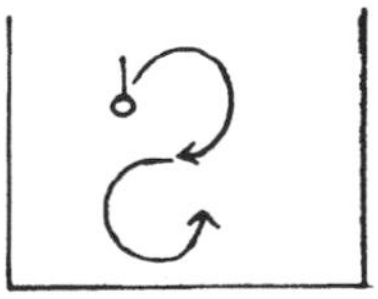

1,2

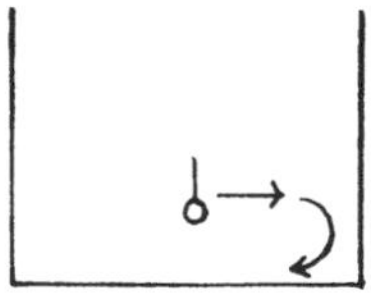

3,4

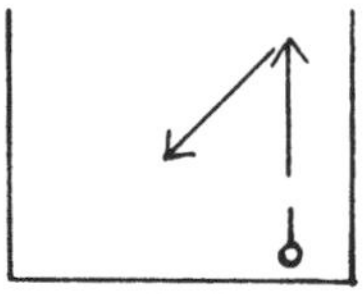

5,6

Exercise Sheet - 10

## SPIRAL PATHS

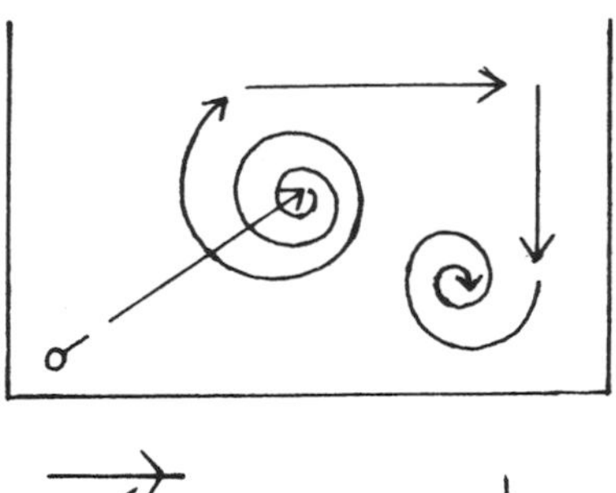

Notate with forward travelling the appropriate paths which will produce the floor plan illustrated here. Remember that spiralling takes time!

If a path sign needs to be continued from one staff to the next, place a caret: > at the end of the sign, as in Ex. a, and another caret at the beginning of the repeat of the path sign in the next staff, Ex. b. Carets have the meaning of 'the same'.

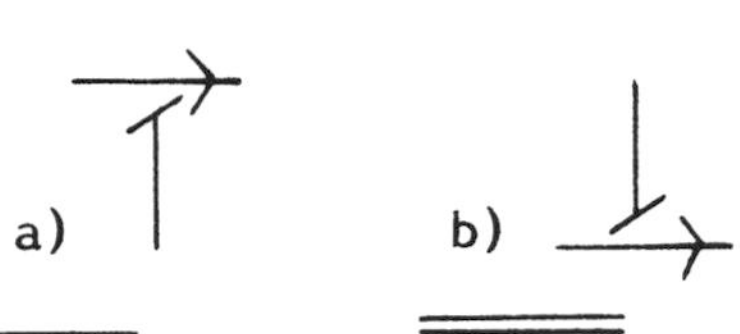


4 8 12 16

3 7 11 15

2 6 10 14

1 5 9 13

YOUR MOVE - Chapter 3 Name:

Exercise Sheet - 11

## TRAVELLING WITH TURNING

Although turning while travelling on a straight path should produce only a straight line on the floor plan, the addition of loops is a useful device to indicate the direction and number of revolutions. Such use is a practical convention which is not always used.

Notate the movements which will produce the floor plans below. Include degrees for circular paths and for the turns needed to face the new direction to start the next path.

4 ______ 8 ______ 12 ______ 16 ______

3 ______ 7 ______ 11 ______ 15 ______

2 ______ 6 ______ 10 ______ 14 ______

1 ______ 5 ______ 9 ______ 13 ______

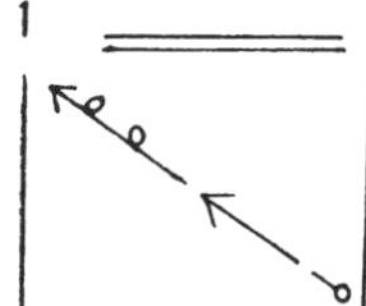
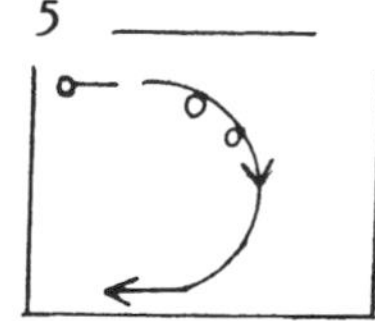
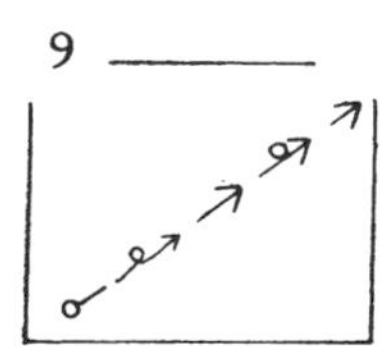
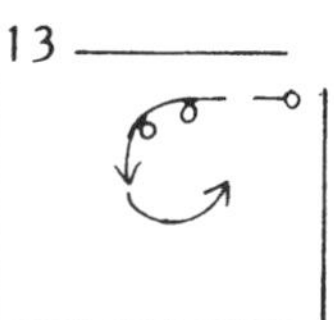

 Name:

Exercise Sheet - 12

## REVOLVING WHILE TRAVELLING

Notate the travelling patterns as described below following the additional information given in the floor plans. Draw in the floor plans.

Travel to the left with a half turn left.

2

Travel forward with 3/4 turn to left.

4

Travel forward in a half circle CCW while also turning 1/2 to right.

6

While travelling to the right perform a half turn to the right.

1

Travel forward with 3/4 turn to right.

3

Travel forward a full circle CW while also turning 1/2 to the right.

5

Start of 1.

Start of 3.

Start of 5.

Name:

Exercise Sheet - 13

## AERIAL STEPS

1. Explain the idea behind the symbol for a spring: ( )
   What do the parts of it represent?

2. Notate the following:

1 Spring before travelling forward . . . . .

2 Three springs while turning to the right

3 Spring, then hold still.

4 Clockwise circle ending with a spring

5 Four consecutive springs

6 One spring turning, then stillness

7 Go down . . Spring ending down Stillness

8 Spring as you start to travel backward

 Name:

Exercise Sheet - 14

## VARIATIONS IN SIZE OF SPRING

Notate the following:

A. Two inward spirals which start and end with a small spring.

B. A large spring followed by two rebound small springs, a pivot turn, then repeat, turning the other way.

C. Four small springs turning around yourself, one large spring, then stillness. Repeat to the other side.

| A | B | C |
|---|---|---|
| 4 | 4 | 4 |
| 3 | 3 | 3 |
| 2 | 2 | 2 |
| 1 | 1 | 1 |

YOUR MOVE - Chapter 5 Name:

Exercise Sheet - 15

## DIRECTIONS IN EVERYDAY LIFE

1. List four objects which have no front or back.

2. List three objects which have no up and down (no right way up).

3. How did the term 'upstage' get its name?

4. Which step patterns (footwork) best suit sideward travelling?

5. Give two examples in which the word 'up' is used in a relative sense, i.e. not toward the ceiling or sky, and explain how or why the word is used for that particular meaning.

6. Give two everyday examples of use of the word 'down' which do not refer to a motion toward the floor. How is the word used in these contexts?

7. What animal, insect, etc. is able easily to travel sideward? List as many as you can.

 Name:

Exercise Sheet- 16

DIRECTION - DEFINITION OF SPACE

1. What is the Kinesphere? Where in the room is it located?

2. If movement which travels is called 'locomotor' movement, what is the name given to movements around your center which stay on the spot?

3. What is the meaning of 'sagittal'?

4. How is the center of direction: ▯ used expressively or practically?

5. What does the difference in length of a direction symbol indicate?

6. Write the following signs:

A. The basic shape for direction

B. 'Any direction'

C. An action anywhere on the vertical line

D. Any upward direction

E. Any forward level

F. In the upward area

G. In the right side area

H. More or less forward middle

I. Exactly forward middle

 Name:

Exercise Sheet - 17

EXPRESSIVENESS OF DIRECTIONS

1. Give two natural movement expressions which are associated with the following directions:

   A. Up (upward)

   B. Down (downward)

   C. Forward horizontal

   D. Backward

   E. Open sideward

   F. Crossed sideward

2. How can a forward arm gesture toward another person be affected by how the rest of the body is used? Give three examples explaining your choice and the effect produced.

 Name:

Exercise Sheet - 18

## DIRECTIONS AND LEVELS

1. Draw the symbols for the following points, placing the appropriate sign next to the dots.

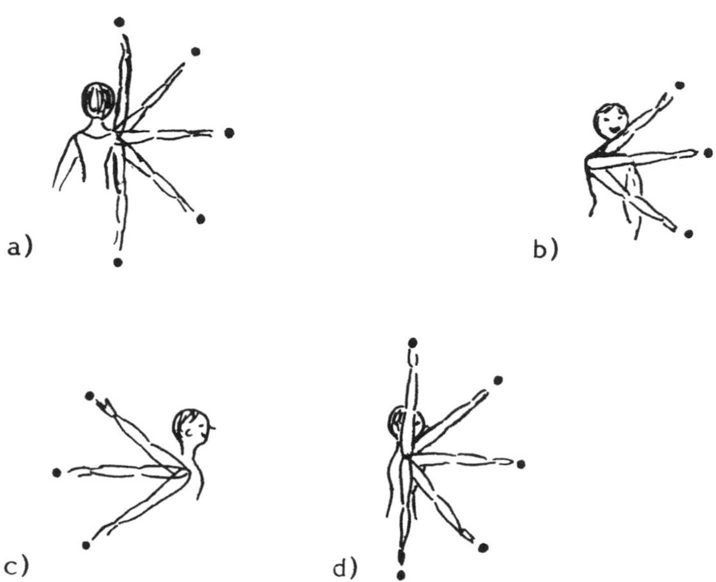


2. Can a performer accurately arrive at an infinite number of points in space? Is there a limit to the number of points for which differences can be observed?

3. Give the general directional indications for:

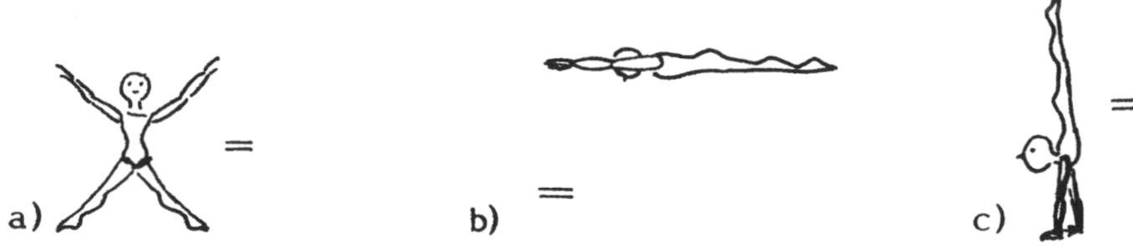

YOUR MOVE - Chapter 5 Name:

Exercise Sheet - 19

## DIRECTIONAL ACTIONS

Notate the following:

Quick left   Stillness   1 ________

Quick right   Stillness   2 ________

Left   Right   3 ________

Left   Sustained rising . . . .   4 ________

Slow lowering backward low . . . . . . . . . . . .   5 ________   6 ________

Slow forward horizontal movement with three evenly spaced accents   7 ________   8 ________

Right low   Left high . . .   9 ________

Left low   Right high . . .   10 ________

Stillness   11 ________

Slow sustained lowering . . . . .   12 ________

Exercise Sheet - 20

## JUMPING, TRAVELLING AND DIRECTIONAL MOVEMENTS

Dance your ideas for the following movement suggestions; then notate the results. Try to indicate a logical timing for the springing patterns you choose.

Combine springs and sideward travelling with sideward leg gestures during the springs.

Springs with forward leg gestures (no travelling) - Travel forward with springs using backward leg gestures. - Travel backward with springs using forward leg gestures.

Use forward and backward gestures in springs and add some travelling forward and backward.

 Name:

Exercise Sheet - 21

## FLEXION, EXTENSION - EVERYDAY ACTIONS

1. Describe two instances when actions of flexing occur in:

   A - Animals (e.g. a hedgehog curled up)

   B - Plants

   C - Humans

2. Describe two instances when actions of extension occur for:

   D - Animals (e.g. a Lippizaner horse at the height of a cabriole)

   E - Plants

   F - Humans

Name:

Exercise Sheet - 22

## FLEXION, EXTENSION - PRACTICAL EXAMPLES

For the following timing is important:

Notate flexion/extension time patterns for the following. Do not be concerned with other elements which would come into a full movement description. Indicate relative timing and directional path (where appropriate) and whether any pauses occur.

A. Sawing wood.

B. Reach up and give a bell rope a sharp pull.

C. Close your hand slowly and gently over a butterfly, then suddenly release it, throwing it into the air.

D. Reach forward and pull the bedclothes up to your chin.

B

D

Add to the flexion/ extension indications any of the paths given above which may be applicable in describing the movement.

A

C

 Name:

Exercise Sheet - 23

## SPRINGS WITH FLEXION AND EXTENSION

1. Notate the following aerial steps taking care to show whether flexion or extension is for the body as a whole or just for the legs.

   Note: ⇑ = both arms. ↿ = left arm. ↾ = right arm.

| A | B | C |
|---|---|---|
| D | E | F |

2. For the following indicate how the state of the body while in the air is different from the state after landing (read up).

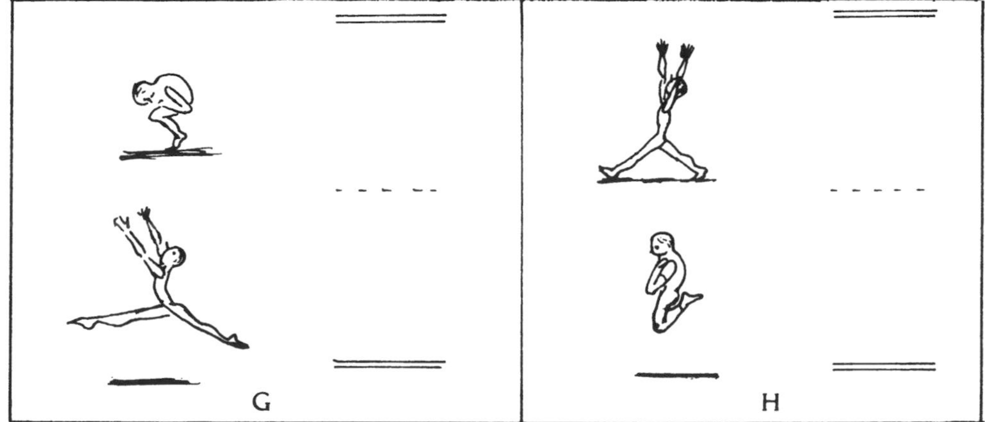

YOUR MOVE - Chapter 7 Name:

Exercise Sheet - 24

## ROTATIONS, TURNS - EVERYDAY EXAMPLES

List four examples of rotations from everyday life under the following types:

1. Horizontal axis: rotation on a lateral plane (e.g. the hands of a clock).

2. Horizontal axis: rotation on a sagittal plane (e.g. the wheels of a car)

3. Vertical axis: rotations on a horizontal plane (e.g. a revolving door)

 Name:

Exercise Sheet - 25

## ROTATIONS, TURNS

Notate the following; give only the signs for the turning actions involved:

A. Turn quickly to see something behind you. Turn back slowly, disappointed.
B. A Cossack does a series of quick, snap turns, first one way, then the other with stops between.
C. A series of pivot turns (pirouettes): 1 turn, 2 turns, 3 turns, then 4 turns. Consider whether the duration for each of these turns will change. (Degrees of turning were given in Chapter Three).
D. A model slowly turns to show off a gown, then she suddenly turns and dashes off having heard the furious voice of her employer.
E. A Whirling Dervish spins endlessly, turning counterclockwise.

B

A C D E

 Name:

Exercise Sheet - 26

## ROTATIONS

Notate the following:

A sudden extension precedes a slow CCW rotation.

B

Flex, log roll, then somersault roll.

D

A cartwheel to the right, a pivot turn, then a cartwheel to the left.

F

Rotate CW very slowly and at the same time flex.

A

A forward somersault roll curled up, stillness, then a backward somersault roll.

C

Only near the end of a slow extension does a CW turn occur.

E

Exercise Sheet - 27

## PARTS OF THE BODY SUPPORTING

Notate the part (or parts) of the body supporting for the illustrations below.

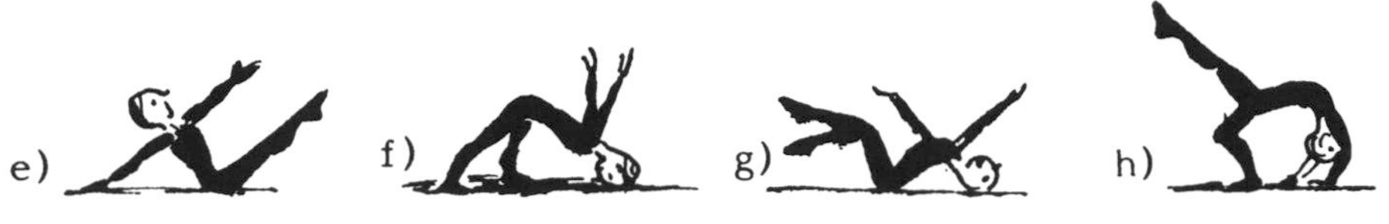

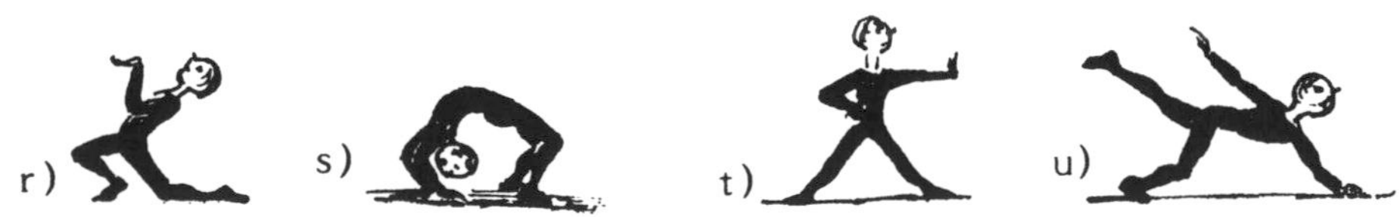

 Name:

Exercise Sheet - 28

## SUPPORTING, CHANGE OF SUPPORT

1. Write the sign for supporting (carrying weight) at 1a. Can it be drawn another way?

1a

1b

2. In the space provided write:
a) a slow transference of weight.
b) two fast transferences.

2a 2b

3. Write the sign for any kind of rolling on the floor.

4. Add indications to this example to show rolling with continuous support.

3 4

5. What is the difference between 5a, 5b and 5c?

5a  5b  5c

6. a) Notate a whole body action forward low accompanied by one transference of weight.
b) Notate a forward low step on the left foot.

7. How is the supporting bow drawn when two parts support at the same time?

6a 6b

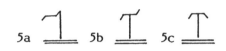

8. Write in the following signs:

| Either foot: | Right foot: | Both feet: | Left foot: |
|---|---|---|---|
| Either knee: | Right knee: | Both knees: | Left knee: |
| Either hand: | Right hand: | Both hands: | Left hand: |

YOUR MOVE - Chapter 8 Name:

Exercise Sheet - 29

## SUPPORTING, CHANGE OF SUPPORT

1. Notate the following supporting situations:

A. Kneeling

B. Sitting

C. Lying

D. Lying on the back

E. Lying on the front

F. Lying on the right side

G. Lying on the left side

H. Supporting on both knees and one hand

I. Supporting on right knee and left foot

J. Supporting on left knee and right foot

2. a) Notate a circular path which occurs with five steps starting on the left foot.
   b) Notate a slow contraction during which steps occur.
   c) Notate a slow extension which starts with three steps, L,R,L.

A

B

C

Exercise Sheet - 30

## VARIATIONS IN SUPPORTS

Describe what is happening in the examples here: ( ∾ means to release, let go).

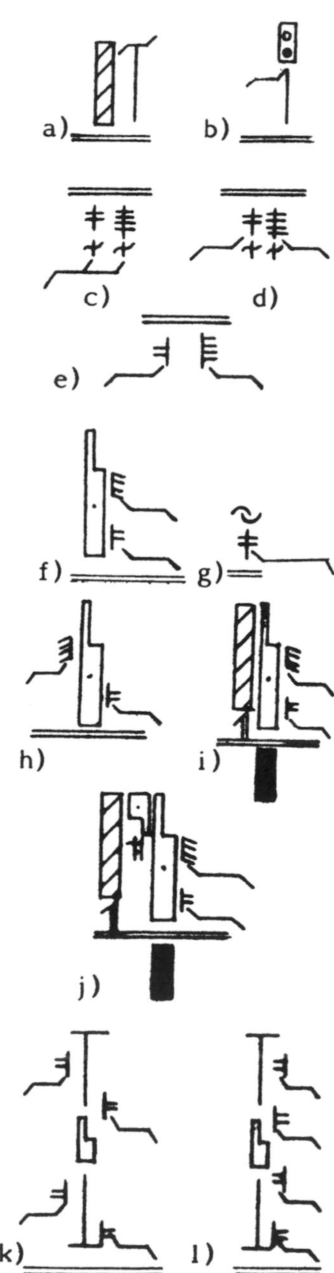

Name:

Exercise Sheet - 31

## BALANCE

1. List three examples of movement skills in gymnastics or sports or instances in well known ballets where sustained balance is featured.

2. Draw at A a figure in profile doing a hand stand which is on balance. At B draw an off balance handstand. Illustrate by a dotted line where you think the vertical line of balance is.
   In C place a dot (●) where you think the center of gravity lies.

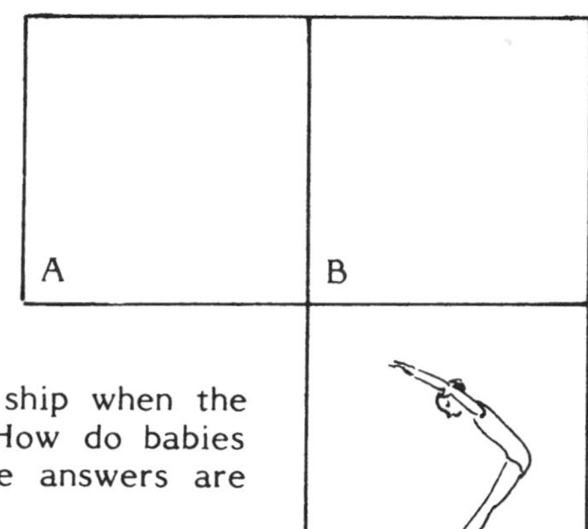


3. How do people walk on board ship when the weather is rough, and why? How do babies and elderly people walk? The answers are all the same!

4. Using the sign for the center of gravity and the appropriate pin, ⊥ , ⊢ , ⊤ , etc. indicate what happens when an untrained person performs the following:

   a) a forward leg kick (grand battement)

   b) an unfolding leg extension to the right

   c) a deep knee bend (grand plié)

5. Describe what is happening in 5a, 5b, and 5c.

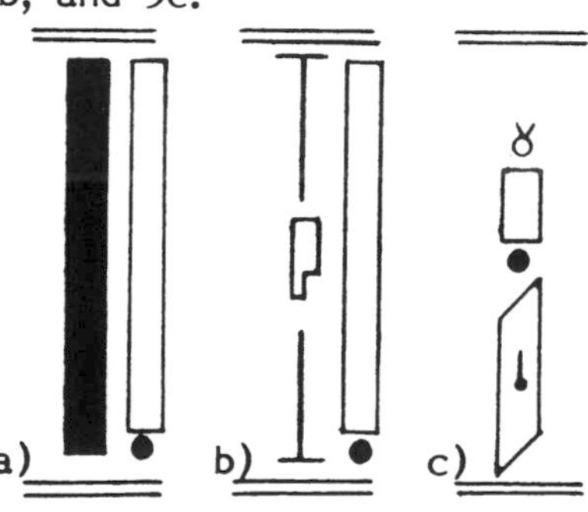

YOUR MOVE - Chapter 9 Name:

Exercise Sheet - 32

LOSS OF BALANCE STUDY

Taking movement ideas from the dance studies given on page 119 and 123, compose and notate a sequence using slight falling and also true loss of balance. Be sure to cancel any retained falling indications.

6 12

5 11

4 10 16

3 9 15

2 8 14

1 7 13

Exercise Sheet - 33

## FALLING

1. Add the necessary indications to state the following:

A

A tombé into a step on the right foot

B

Travelling forward with the weight shifted forward

C

A slow step forward on the left foot, the weight shifted backward

D

Travelling backward with slight loss of balance

E

Falling backward

F

Center of gravity leads into circling clockwise

G

At the end of a turn fall to the right

H

A step on the R foot cancels a forward fall

2. Describe what is happening in this sequence (note that directions are left open).

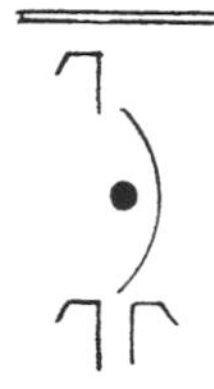

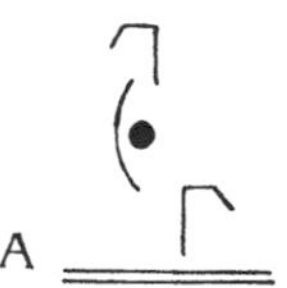

A

B



c

 Name:

Exercise Sheet - 34

## RELATING

1. What basic forms of action (types of movement) may occur in connection with relating, to produce some form of relationship.

2. Why have special signs been devised to indicate the various ways of relating?

3. What is meant by mutual relating?

4. Notate the following:

a) A is aware of B

b) B is aware of A

c) A and B are aware of each other

d) D addresses E

e) E addresses D

f) D addresses E, but E is only aware of D

5. Notate the following:

A circular path ending addressing a chair

Any path away from your partner ending center stage

A spiral path addressing each corner of the room as you pass it

YOUR MOVE - Chapter 10 Name:

Exercise Sheet - 35

## NEAR, TOUCH, GRASP

1. a) What is the sign for nearness?

   b) Show how this sign is modified to indicate enclosing nearness:

2. For touching, how is the bow modified to show the active part? Give an example to illustrate your answer.

3. What is the difference between: 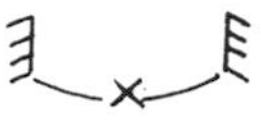 and 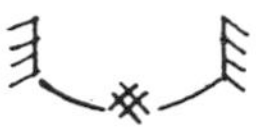 ?

4. Notate the following:

a) A forward gesture ends near a lamp

b) Your head lowers forward to touch the table

c) Both hands hide a flower without touching it

d) Your head touches your knees

e) Your index finger touches your nose

f) A cat curls around your ankle

g) Your R elbow grasps the lamp post

h) Your L hand grasps your R knee

i) Your hands grasp your elbows

 Name:

Exercise Sheet - 36

CARRYING, GRASPING

1. List three everyday examples in which you are involved in the activity of carrying.

2. What is the difference between a) [symbol] b) [symbol] ?

3. a) What is the indication for carrying with grasp?

   b) What are the three ways in which you can show the active person or part? Which is the more usual way? Give examples to illustrate your answer.

4. Notate the following descriptions:

a) You are wearing a tiara (carrying it on your head)

b) You are standing on a tray

c) Kneeling on a chair

d) A hat is on the floor, stand on the hat

e) You are carrying a child (G) by the waist

f) Stand on a book

g) Carry an umbrella in your left hand

h) A is sitting on B's knees

YOUR MOVE - Chapter 10 Name:

Exercise Sheet - 37

INDICATIONS FOR RELATING

1. Now that you are familiar with the different forms of relating, list them below from the slightest to the greatest involvement or concern with a person or object.

a) b) c) d)

e) f) g) h)

i) j) k) l)

2. a) How long does a particular statement of 'relating' usually last?

   b) How do you show that a stated relationship is to be maintained (retained, kept, held - which word is suitable)?

   c) What sign is used for cancellation?

   d) If a passing relationship (a passing relating) is to continue, how is this shown?

3. Describe what is happening in the following:

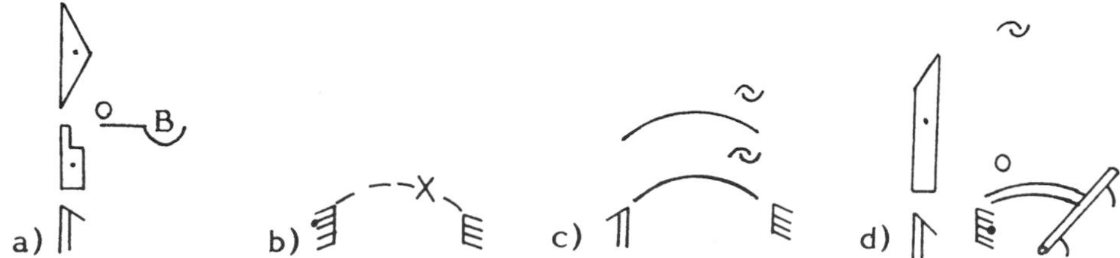

 Name:

Exercise Sheet - 38

## PASSING (SLIDING) RELATIONSHIPS

1. Notate the following:

A
Glancing along a car

B
Hand slides along leg

C
Grasping and rubbing a stick

D
Feet sliding on floor

E
Hand brushes table three times

F
Hand tests the smoothness of whole table top

G
Index finger tests wet paint on door twice

H
Pass hand close to face

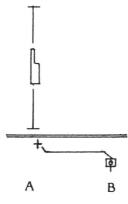

I

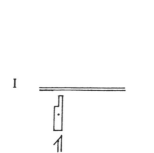

Right hand touches left shoulder, then slides down left arm as right arm extends

J

A B

A slides down B's back on her hips

YOUR MOVE - Chapter 11 Name:

Exercise Sheet - 39

PART LEADING

Notate the following movements:

A

A path sideward led by the right hip

B

Lowering is led by both shoulders

C

A forward path led by the front of the waist

D

Turning left led by the left shoulder

E

Right palm and sole of left foot lead a forward movement

F

A double turn to the right led by the right thumb edge

G

A backward path led by the pelvis

H

A path forward led by the toes

I

Backward circling CW led by the back of the chest

 Name:

Exercise Sheet - 40

## RESULTANT, PASSIVE MOVEMENTS

Notate the following:

1.

As the body lowers the arms passively flex

2.

A B

A is sitting on B's shoulder. As he travels forward she is carried along

3.

A turn to the right causes the arms to 'fling' out to the sides

4.

A B

A's hand is on B's shoulder. As A circles clockwise B is passively turned

5.

Your right hand grasps your left hand and your right arm raises your left arm up

6. A B

Facing each other, A pushes B away (contacting the front of his chest). B nearly falls and passively travels backward

 Name:

Exercise Sheet - 41

## ONE-SIDED GESTURES

Notate the following:

1 As you travel forward the right side of the body gestures backward.

2 A forward gesture for the left side of the body precedes a circular path.

3 As you lower the whole body the right side gestures up.

4 Left side gestures side low then forward low lead into a pivot turn to the right

5 The right side of the body contracts while the left side extends.

6 The left side contracts while the right side extends.

7 A general forward action Right side forward

8 Left side forward Left side across to right side direction

 Name:

Exercise Sheet - 42

## PATHS FOR GESTURES

1. What is the significance of the sign: o added to a path sign to indicate a path for gestures?

2. Notate the following (all are for gestures):

A Straight path gesture

B Straight path upward

C Arc circling clockwise

D Forward sagittal path

E Left leg circling clockwise

F Right arm circling CCW

G Straight path forward for the right arm

H Lateral circle to left for left arm

I Travel to right while arms swing laterally to left.

J Forward sagittal arm circles while travelling backward

K Arms perform four CW circles while you circle clockwise.

Exercise Sheet - 43

## GATHER, SCATTER

Notate the following:

C. Travel sideward right first scattering with right arm, then gather with left arm

F. A scattering action for the left leg

I. A slow scattering action addressing person B

B. Overlapping gathering, left then right, while turning CW

E. A gathering action for the right leg

H. Scatter while jumping, gather as you land and after landing

A. While sinking gathering may be with either side

D. Three sudden scattering actions while rising

G. Gather with right hand then left; scatter with right, then left

YOUR MOVE - Chapter 13 Name:

Exercise Sheet - 44

DIAGONAL TRAVELLING; CONSTANT DIRECTIONS

1. The instruction "Travel diagonally" is open to three different interpretations, what are they?

2. Write the key for the Constant Directions:
What is the logic of this sign?

3. Does ☑ mean the physical right-front corner of the room? Explain your answer.

4. Write in the appropriate front signs here: → (audience)

5. Do these front signs change depending on where in the room you are standing?

6. Draw in the right arm for the figures below following the instruction given in the notation. Remember the top of a sheet of paper is considered to represent the front of the room (stage).

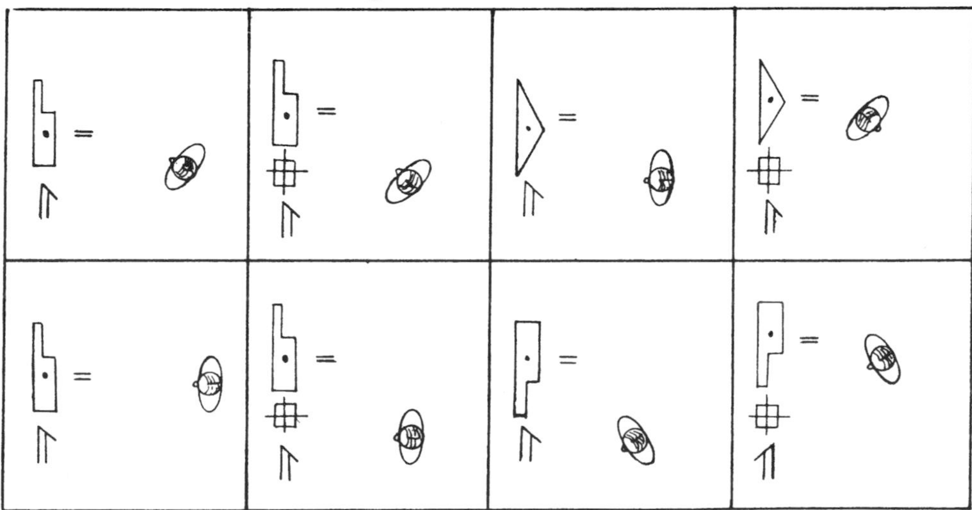

 Name:

Exercise Sheet - 45

## AERIAL STEPS: THE FIVE BASIC FORMS

A. Terms used in everyday life should not be taken literally. Write what you judge to be the form of spring used in the following:

1. A bird hopping on the ground:
2. A grasshopper getting out of the way:
3. A frog leaping from lilypad to lilypad:
4. The preparatory spring onto the springboard before vaulting over the horse:
5. A boy jumping over a fence to get away:
6. A child skipping rope:
7. An athlete performing a long jump:
8. A runner going over a hurdle:
9. Children leapfrogging:

B. When is a skip (a true skip) followed by a step used to gain momentum?

C. Which of the five basic forms is best suited to:

a) travelling (covering horizontal distance)?

b) springing high (covering vertical distance)?

D. For those with Classical Ballet training: to which basic form do the following ballet steps belong? (Refer to pages 193-195 in Your Move.)

1. pas de chat:
2. cabriole:
3. brisé:
4. temps de cuisse:
5. pas de poisson:
6. brisé volé:
7. demi-contretemps:
8. a sprung coupé:
9. saut de basque:
10. temps de fleche:

A temps de trip following a chat de pas.

 Name:

Exercise Sheet - 46

TWISTS, TWISTING

Name, describe or find clippings from newspapers or magazines of ten typical examples in which twisting of some kind occurs. State the type of movement (the field of movement discipline) from which each comes, e.g. wrestling, skating, and identify which parts of the body are twisting. If a limb is twisting state whether it is twisting in or out.

 Name:

Exercise Sheet - 47

## ROTATIONS, TWISTS

Notate the following in the spaces provided:

A. Vigorously saying "No!"

B. Shaking with the cold (shivers).

C. Turn the head away slowly in disgust.

D. Parallel leg rotations.

E. Symmetrical leg rotations.

F. Gesture of hands saying "I have no idea" or "I have no money".

G. Head turns one way while the torso twists the other way.

H. During a slow twist stretch at first, then gradually contract.

(◇ means keep the eyes looking in the same direction despite rotations)

A B C D

E F G H

 Name:

Exercise Sheet - 48

## ROTATIONS, TWISTS

Notate the following:

C.

Twist the body to be able to look behind you

F.

The Shimmy (pelvic rotations while lowering whole body)

I.

Show-off walk (twist chest side to side)

B.

Parallel leg rotations producing travelling to left

E.

Roll to the outside of your feet (inversion) then roll to the inside (eversion)

H.

Arms akimbo (hands on hips, arms rotated so elbows are out)

A.

The right arm rotates inward in one piece

D.

Shake an imaginary bracelet down your arm

G.

Charleston Walk (leg turns in on step, out after the step

Name:

Exercise Sheet - 49

## CONTRACTING, FOLDING

The figure drawings here illustrate various flexed states for the legs. To arrive at these positions it is likely that a contraction or a folding has taken place. Decide logically which each should be and give the sign for the correct form of flexion. **Degree of flexion is not important;** it is the form (contraction or folding) that is required.

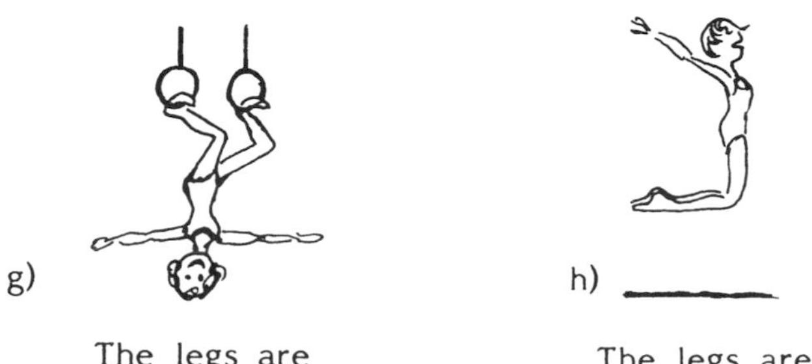

Exercise Sheet - 50

## CONTRACTING, FOLDING

Here are examples of arm and torso flexions which are more likely in the context to have resulted from either contracting or folding (arching). Indicate for each which form of flexion has taken place. It is not important to give the degree of contracting or folding, it is the form which is important.

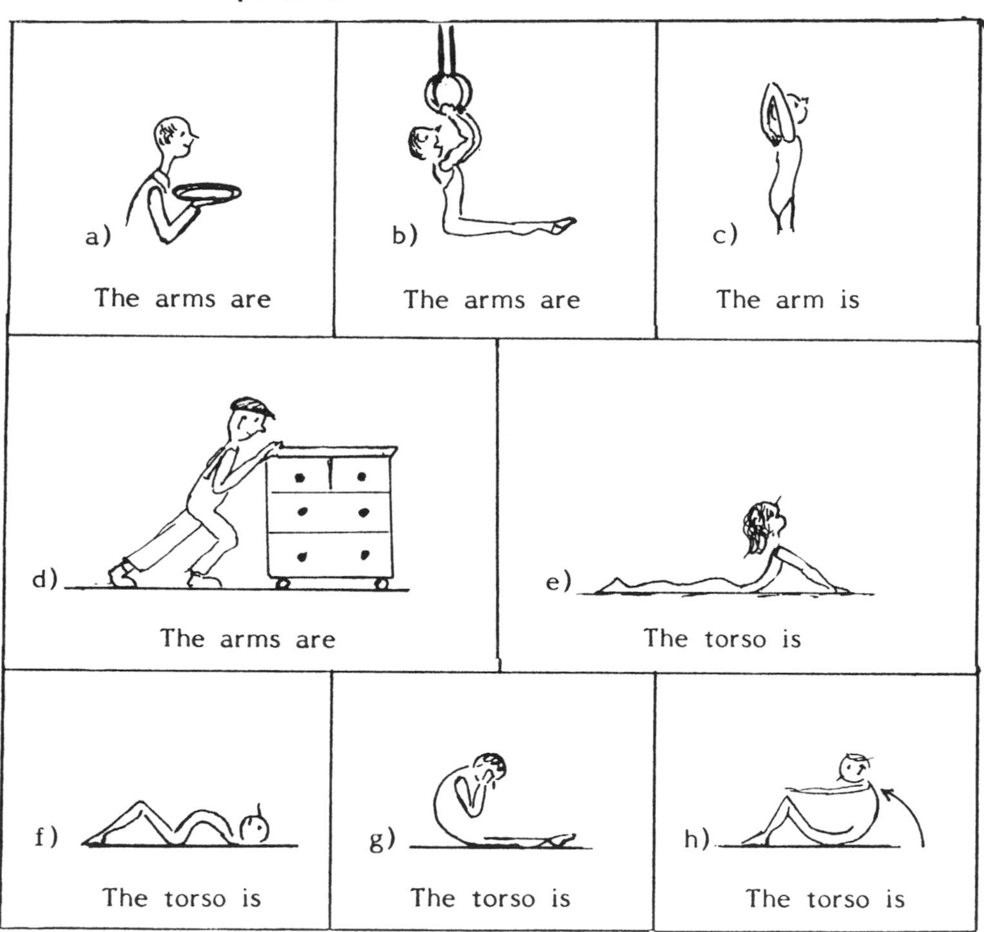

 Name:

Exercise Sheet - 51

## CONTRACTION, ELONGATION

1. When a limb or the torso contracts, what path in space does the extremity describe?

2. Does the spatial relationship between the extremity and the base of the limb change?

3. What part 'bulges out' when a contraction occurs:

a) in the leg b) in the arm c) in the spine d) in the hand

4. Write contraction and direction for the following figures:

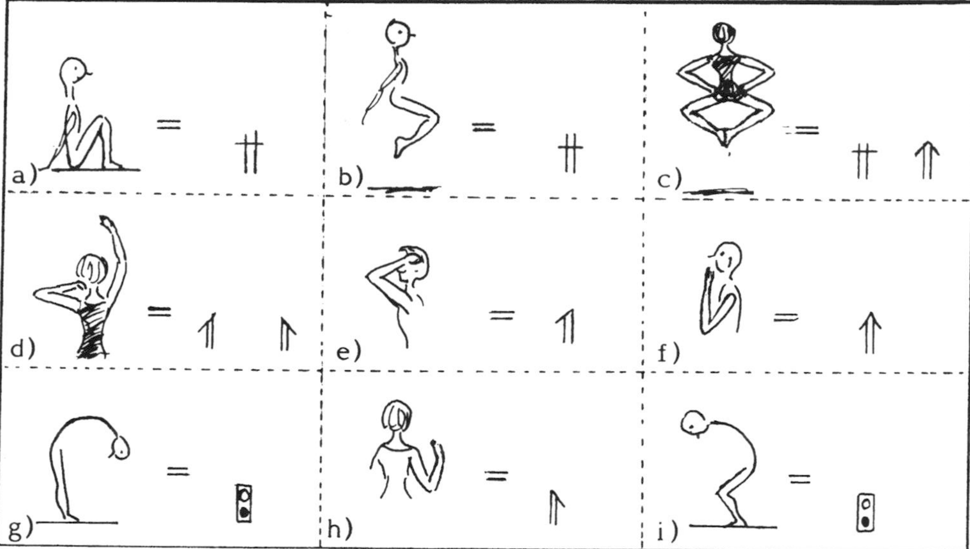


5. Notate the direction in which the limb will elongate (keeping the same spatial direction):

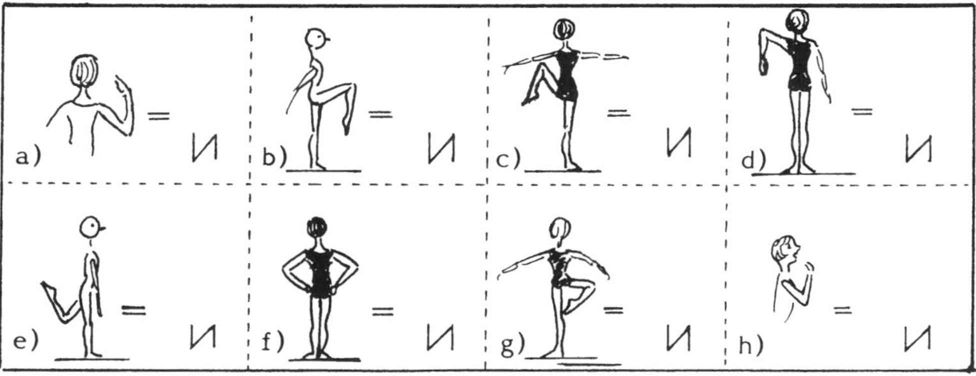

Exercise Sheet - 52

SITUATIONS IN MEETING

If G, ♁ , and ♁ represent a girl, and B, ♁ , and ♁ represent a boy, write the appropriate meeting lines under the floor plan for the stated relationships of the two people. In the floor plan draw the appropriate pins to show the same relationship in a different room orientation. The answer for a) shows one possible solution but the performers could be facing any of the eight directions in the room.

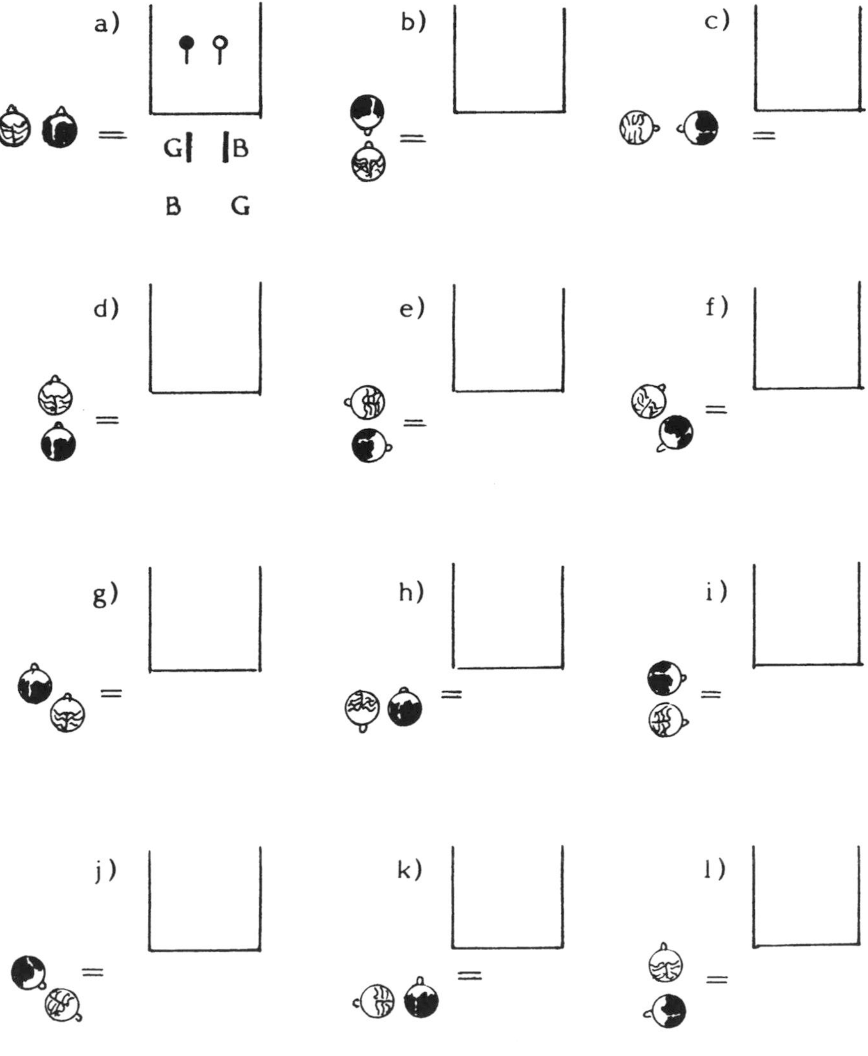

Name:

Exercise Sheet - 53

LOOKING

Notate the following:

A.

"Mercy on us!" (eyes up)

B.

"I've got the wrong shoes on!"

C.

Look over your right shoulder

D.

Surreptitiously read paper of person next to you (eyes only)

E.

Look at hands

F.

Thoughtful. (tilt head, eyes up to side)

G.

Wistful. (tilt head, eyes up to same side)

H.

Snooty. (head backward, eyes forward)

I.

A slow turn of the head which ends looking at partner

J.

Watching a tennis match

K.

Watching a puppy running around your feet

L.

Examining a totem pole top to bottom

 Name:

Exercise Sheet - 54

DESTINATION, MOTION

1. Make a list of eight different everyday examples of destinational movements.

2. List which of the Prime Actions are destinational by nature.

3. Make a list of eight different everyday examples of motion.

4. List which Prime Actions are motion by nature.

5. Describe the affinities which exist between motion and destination and aspects of time, space and dynamics:

| | TIME | SPACE | DYNAMICS |
|---|---|---|---|
| MOTION | | | |
| DESTINATION | | | |

YOUR MOVE - Chapter 18 Name:

Exercise Sheet - 55

## DESTINATION, MOTION

1. Notate the following: (Note: D of P = direction of progression)

A. Motion of stretching

B. End stretched

C. Motion of flexing

D. End flexed

E. Toward ▨

F. Arrive at ▨

G. Approach ■

H. Arrive at ■

I. D of P

J. D of P

K. D of P sinking

L. D of P rising

2. Notate the movement illustrated:

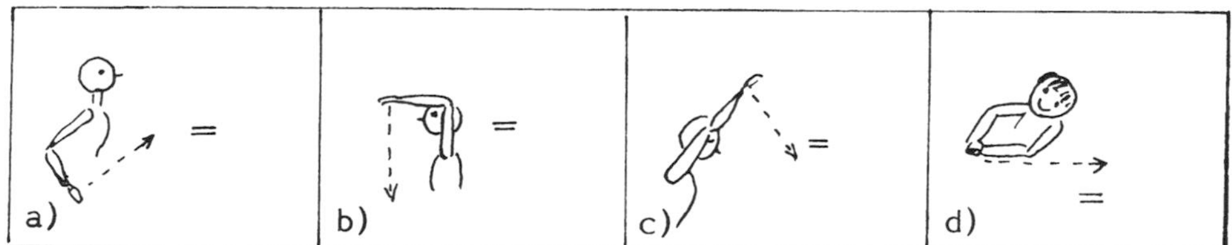


3. Give the starting position and notate the main direction which the limb is approaching.

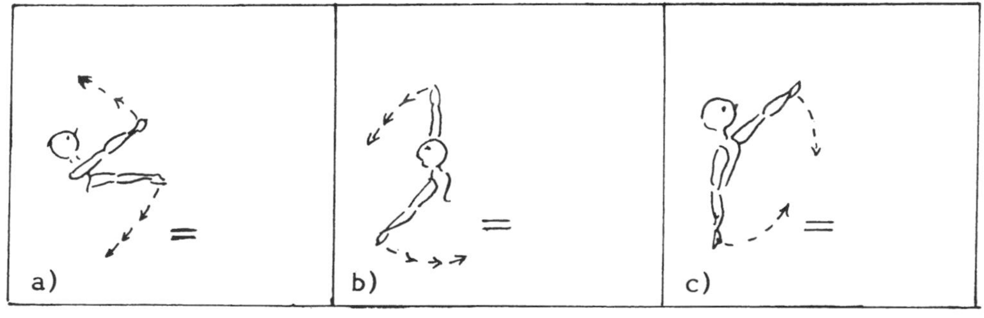

 Name:

Exercise Sheet - 56

## DESTINATION, MOTION

For questions 1 to 5 tick the correct box or fill in the answer:

1. For gestures, a direction symbol indicates: motion ☐, destination ☐

2. For travelling, " " " " " ☐ " ☐

3. A gesture toward a main direction is written as:

   a) ☐ b) ☐ c) ☐ a)  b)  c)

4. An arrow indicates:

5. The arrow is ☐, is not ☐ turned to point into the spatial direction travelled.

6. Notate the following:

a) Arrive down

b) Move toward down

c) Downward direction of progression

7. Describe the following:

a)

b)

c)

d)

YOUR MOVE - Chapter 18 Name:

Exercise Sheet - 57

MINOR DIRECTIONAL DISPLACEMENTS

1. How are minor displacements indicated?

2. Write in the appropriate pins which are the equivalent to these main directions:

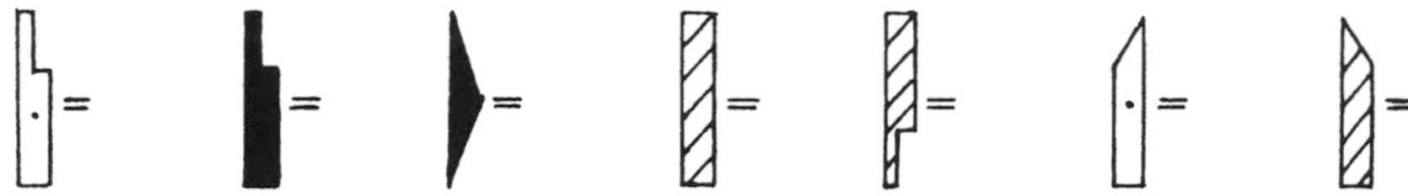

3. Write in the appropriate main direction signs which are the equivalent of these pins:

= = = = = = =

4. Match up the appropriate letter (A,B,C,etc.) to the form of movement indicated in the following examples:

A - Directional destination

B Movement toward a directional destination

C - Direction of the progression

D - Minor displacements

E - Sustained minor displacements

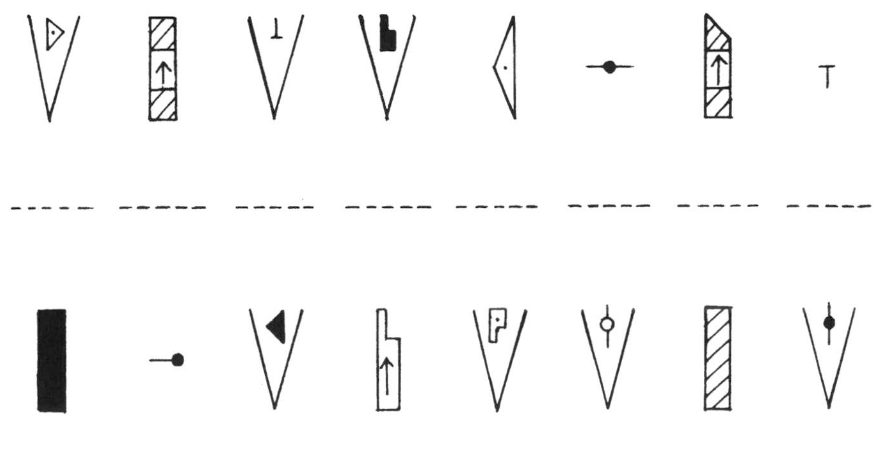

 Name:

Exercise Sheet - 58

## DIRECTIONS - TILTING

Notate the following sequences using your own choice of directions and levels in interpreting the descriptions.

**A**

1. Torso tilts before travelling.
2. Torso tilts slowly all during travelling.
3. Torso tilts after travelling.

**B**

1. Right arm takes a direction — Stillness
2. Left arm takes a direction — Stillness
3. Both arms take a direction

**C**

1. A general movement forward low, both arms take the direction back high
2. A general movement back high, right arm takes the direction forward low
3. A general movement R side low, chest tilts left side high.

**D**

1. Chest tilting in high level: Fwd. R side Back L side
2. Head tilting in high level: Fwd. R side Back L side

 Name:

Exercise Sheet - 59

## SHIFTING BODY AREAS

Notate the following:

1. Look at B, then shift head forward (to peer at B)

2. "Can't hear!" (shift head to right side)

3. "How horrid!" (shift head backward)

4. "Who, me?" (guiltily) (chest shift backward, head forward)

5. Army stance (chest shifted forward, head pulled back)

6. Eavesdropping (head shifts side, then chest shifts to same side)

7. Travel to right while pelvis shifts from side to side

8. Chest shifts to right, to center, to left, then to center

9. Starting to left pelvis shifts in a clockwise circle

10. Head shifts forward and backward

 Name:

Exercise Sheet - 60

## CHOICE OF KEY

Notate the most obvious directional description for the designated limbs in the following examples, stating the key you have chosen.